JUV/E8 Patterson, Lillie.
PZ
7   The jack-o'lantern
.P2768 trick
Jac   4.48

Cop.2

DATE			
		DISCARD	

© THE BAKER & TAYLOR CO.

The Jack-o'-Lantern Trick

The Jack o' Lantern Trick

By Lillie Patterson

Drawings by William Hutchinson

GARRARD PUBLISHING COMPANY
CHAMPAIGN, ILLINOIS

To
Alex Peterson, Jr.

Library of Congress Cataloging in Publication Data

Patterson, Lillie.
    The Jack-o'-lantern trick.

    (First holiday books)
    SUMMARY: When unfriendly Indians threaten them and
their home, two pioneer girls use their Halloween jack-o-
lanterns to good advantage.
    [1. Halloween—Fiction. 2. Frontier and pioneer
life—Fiction] 1. Hutchinson, William, 1925-
ll. Title. lll. Series.
PZ7.P2768Hal   [E]   78-11307
ISBN 0-8116-7250-6

Acknowledgment:

This story is based upon "The Indians and the
Jack-o'-Lanterns" from *Pilgrim Stories and Plays*
by Margaret B. Pumphrey. Copyright 1912, 1932
by Rand McNally & Company.

The Jack-o'-Lantern Trick

It was Halloween morning
on the little farm.
"Come here, girls,"
father called
to Fancy and Hester.
The girls came running.

"Your mother and I
are going to the village,"
he said.
"It is a long way,
so we may not
get back home tonight.
Will you be afraid
to stay alone?"

"Oh, no,"
answered Fancy and Hester.
"There are things
you can do
while we are gone,"
said their mother.
"Please sweep and dust
the house."

"And you can bring in
the ripe pumpkins
from the field,"
father added.
"Pile them with the others,
beside the potato pit."
The pit was a deep hole
where potatoes were stored
in the winter.
"We will clean the house
and bring in the pumpkins
while you are gone,"
the girls said.
"Each of you may have one,"
said their mother.
"You can make
jack-o'-lanterns for Halloween."

Mother and father said good-bye
to the girls.
They climbed into their wagon.
The horse started
on the long trip
to the village.

The two children
watched their parents
until they were out of sight.
Then Fancy and Hester
went back to the log house
their father had built.
Their nearest neighbors
were Indians
who lived in the woods.
The Indians were friendly.
They often came to the house
to bring corn and meat.
The girls swept and dusted.
They put more wood
on the fire.
Then they hung a big pot
over the flames.

They cooked some meat and corn
for their dinner.
After they had eaten,
they washed the dishes.

Then the girls
ran to the field.
They rolled
the big orange pumpkins
to the pile
beside the potato pit.

By late afternoon
all the pumpkins were in.
Fancy and Hester
sat down to rest
behind the pile of pumpkins.

After a while
Fancy said to Hester,
"Let's make
our jack-o'-lanterns now."
The girls got knives.
Each took a pumpkin.
They cut out the inside
of the pumpkins.

Fancy watched while Hester
cut two round holes
for eyes.
Then Hester cut
a wide hole for the mouth.
She cut some big ugly teeth
in her pumpkin.
Soon both girls
had finished making
their jack-o'-lanterns.
They stood back
to look at them.
"They are frightening,
aren't they?"
The girls giggled.

"Let's take them inside,"
Fancy said to Hester.
"I will find some candles.
Then we can light
our jack-o'-lanterns."
The girls took
the pumpkins into the house.

"While you find the candles,
I'll put some straw
in the potato pit,"
Hester told Fancy.
"Father will be pleased.
He always
lines the pit with straw
to keep the potatoes dry."

Hester sang to herself
as she took some straw
from a pile nearby.
She jumped into the pit
to spread the straw.
Suddenly she stopped.
Hester heard voices
coming from the path.
"Father and mother
have come back,"
she thought happily.
Hester looked over
the top of the pit.
She was ready to climb out
and run to meet them.
But her happiness
changed quickly to fear.

There,
at the edge of the woods,
stood two Indians!
Their faces were covered
with red and black paint.
They carried bows and tomahawks.

Hester knew in a minute
that they were not
friendly Indians.
These Indians
were on the warpath!
She dropped down
in the bottom of the pit
where she would not be seen.

Then she thought about her sister
alone in the house.
Hester's heart began to pound.
What would happen
if Fancy came out
and the Indians saw her?
Hester looked
over the top of the pit again.
The Indians were whispering
and pointing toward the house.
Then suddenly,
they disappeared into the woods.
Hester ran into the house.
She shut and locked the door.

"There were Indians outside!"
she whispered to Fancy.
"What shall we do?"

Fancy laughed.
"Indians won't hurt us.
You know
that they come often
to bring us gifts."

"These are not
the friendly Indians we know,"
Hester told her sister.
"These are Indians
from another tribe.
They had on war paint.
They may come back tonight
and carry us away.
Maybe they will kill us."
"Oh!" cried Fancy.
"We can't stay in here.
They might
burn down our house!
What if mother and father
don't come back tonight?"
The two frightened girls
hugged each other.

"What will we do?"
Hester asked Fancy.
"The best place to hide
is in the potato pit,"
Fancy said.
Then Hester had another idea.

"We'll take our jack-o'-lanterns
with us," she said.
Quickly
Fancy lighted the candle
in her pumpkin.
Hester got more candles.

Then the two girls
slipped out of the door
with their jack-o'-lanterns.
They got into
the potato pit.
Both girls were shaking
with fear.

They were afraid
that the Indians
had seen them.
But no Indians came.
Fancy whispered to Hester,
"They didn't see us."
The girls were quiet
for a long time.
Then Hester said,
in a low voice,
"The Indians
don't know about Halloween.
When they see our lanterns,
they may think
that they are evil spirits."
"It's our only chance,"
Fancy whispered back.

The girls
hardly dared to breathe.
There, in the potato pit,
they waited.
Hour after hour passed
and nothing happened.
At last,
they heard soft footsteps.

In the dark night,
the footsteps were coming
toward the house.
They could hear the Indians,
creeping nearer, nearer.
"Now!" whispered Fancy.
Quickly the girls put
their jack-o'-lanterns
on the edge of the pit.

The Indians stopped.
They looked in wonder.
The glowing eyes
and ugly mouths
looked like monsters
in the night.
With loud cries
the Indians ran back
into the woods.

The girls
hugged each other happily.

It was a long time
before they dared to talk.
Finally, Hester said,
"The jack-o'-lanterns saved us!"
Fancy laughed.
"Those Indians have not learned
that jack-o'-lanterns are fun!"